At the End of the Road

My Autobiography Part 2

Bud W. Hunton

THE AUTOBIOGRAPHY OF BUD W. HUNTON

PART 2: AT THE END OF THE ROAD

Bud W. Hunton

Author's Tranquility Press
ATLANTA, GEORGIA

Bud W. Hunton/Author's Tranquility Press
3800 Camp Creek Pkwy SW Bldg. 1400-116 #1255
Atlanta, GA 30331, USA
www.authorstranquilitypress.com

Ordering Information:
Quantity sales. Special discounts are available on quantity purchases by corporations, associations, and others. For details, contact the "Special Sales Department" at the address above.

The Autobiography of Bud W. Hunton Part 2: At The End Of The Road / Bud W. Hunton
Paperback: 978-1-966088-58-5
eBook: 978-1-966088-59-2

Acknowledgments

I would like to pay homage and recognize the following people:

- All my former navy shipmates that I sailed with on various ships, navy hospital corpsman that I served with ashore and abroad, and my fellow corpsman who died in Vietnam.
- To my relatives throughout the country who have stayed in touch and provided me with words of wisdom especially my youngest daughter Deborah Donchez who has provided moral support to me and my wife of sixty-five years Beverly.
- To my amazing publishers who have provided much-needed advice and support, particularly Honey Evans of Author's Tranquility Press.

Prologue

Part 2 of my autobiography describes my post-military retirement experience, including twenty-one years at Grandview Hospital followed by twenty-two years teaching at Sinclair Community College Dayton, Ohio.

This is a true story of a young boy from Wapakoneta, Ohio. Leaving a rural home to join the Navy at the age of 17, he dropped out of high school with the idea of seeing the world as described by older men who had seen military service. His travels and adventures would span across the Pacific Ocean, Atlantic Ocean, Mediterranean Sea and other areas of the globe. After twenty years of traveling with the Navy, Bud would retire with his wife and four daughters. Travel with his family included moving to a new duty station every eighteen months. Moving was so frequent, that boxes from our previous move were still unpacked when orders to a new duty station were received. In his later years. Although he began his early life as a high school dropout, Bud would write and publish eleven nonfiction books that would relate to his lifetime experiences

During my early teen years, I pumped gas and washed dishes at Goodwin's Bar and Restaurant located in a rural area in what now is known as old Route 33. After moving from the Goodwins property to Wapakoneta, Ohio I also worked part-time at Parker's restaurant on the east side of Wapakoneta. I struggled to stay in high school and eventually dropped out and joined the Navy. Eventually, I ended up with three college degrees and was the author of eleven published books. I owe much of my success to four young draftees who became my "big brothers" shortly after I became a Navy Hospital Corpsman

Chapter 1
Early days of travel

My earliest recollection of traveling is leaving Wapakoneta for the U.S. Naval Training Center at Great Lakes, Illinois. At the age of seventeen. This was an exciting adventure, and I looked forward to seeing other parts of the world. Prior to leaving Wapakoneta, I had worked in a restaurant owned by Margaret (Mag) Goodwin and her husband Bud Goodwin, who was my dad's best friend and my namesake. I washed dishes, pumped gas, and did odd jobs for the Goodwins. Their restaurant included a bar service that was often frequented by young men who had completed military service and would talk to me as I listened to their stories about their military service.

Although my earliest childhood memories consist of sad moments when I was worried about being placed in an orphanage, I was fortunate to meet four college dropouts who were drafted into the Navy around the same time I had enlisted. During the two years I was stationed at the Great Lakes Naval Station and U.S. Naval Hospital Great Lakes, Illinois, these young college-educated men became "big brothers" and helped get me started on a new way of life. I will always remember their kindness.

My first Trip (the beginning of my adventure)

In the summer of 1955, I joined the Navy at the age of 17 left Wapakoneta, Ohio, and traveled to Chicago Illinois by train via the station in Lima, Ohio twelve miles from Wapakoneta. Lima, Ohio was considered a "big city" compared to Wapakoneta. It was where our relatives and friends went shopping on weekends. The Bargain Barn was located on Dixie Highway (old Route 25).

Route 25 (Dixie Highway) was a primary route that existed before Interstate 75. North Dixie Drive is currently located five miles from where I reside. As a young man of sixteen years old, I hitchhiked to

Georgia just for the fun of it with my boyhood friend Jerry Mahaffey. We only stayed for a day or so and then returned to Wapakoneta.

In the next several months while stationed at Great Lakes Naval Station, I would travel to Lima from Chicago on weekends, usually meeting my sister Margaret at the station. I usually wore my navy uniform and was surprised by how friendly people were and offered me free drinks while sitting in the "bar car" where drinks were served. I will never forget the Friday afternoon I met a beautiful young woman who was working full time in Chicago and was headed home to Lima for the weekend. We shared drinks and became very friendly. Upon arrival at the train station, and disembarking the train steps, she asked me if I would like to come over to her apartment for a visit. She asked me this as Aggie was approaching us on the railroad platform.

I was nineteen years old at the time and was young and naïve. I was dumbfounded, astonished, and amazed. I had never been approached sexually by any female in my life. As Aggie and her husband Marion approached us, I was at a loss for words. My female companion realized this and said, have a nice weekend, see you next time. I never met her again.

First trip (continued)

My sister Margaret was given the name Margaret after Margaret Goodwin, wife of Bud Goodwin, my namesake. She adopted the name of Aggie. Not sure why, however, there are at least two people that I know of who have been named after Margaret Goodwin.

Margaret (Maggie) Goodwin, the niece of Margaret Goodwin, was also given this name. Years later I would have to contact relatives of Margaret Goodwin to clarify this. The train station in Lima, Ohio, was a starting point for my travels that would eventually take me around the world. In a few months, I would be traveling on trains throughout Japan.

On my weekends off, I took a train from Chicago to Lima, to visit family and friends or to Terre Haute Indiana to visit with my dad and Tina, who resided in Brazil Indiana at the time. I would spend time with my girlfriend Angie Nichols. On one occasion while headed back to Chicago, I was sitting across the aisle from a small group of nuns. It was late at night and I was exhausted from partying with Dad and his friends. I fell asleep shortly after the train was underway. About an hour or so later I woke up as one of the nuns was covering me with my raincoat that had been lying on the seat next to me. I looked towards them, and they all gave me a big smile.

While at the Great Lakes, Naval base, I received orders to the naval hospital in Yokosuka, Japan. I was given options by the navy to drive, fly, or go by train to California, where I would be flown to Japan. I would be reimbursed regardless of my choice. I chose the train because I did not own a car at the time and wanted to see the country. I was amazed at the scenery from the train window. I had a view of the various landscapes throughout the country from Illinois to California.

The view was breathtaking and impressive for a young man who had very little travel experience. Arriving in California, I was eventually transported to Japan via military transport from Travis Air Force Base to Tokyo, Japan, and then to Yokosuka, Japan.

In the years to come, I would travel the globe to observe the beauty of the world we live in. I would spend two years in Japan before returning to the States and my hometown of Wapakoneta, Ohio.

Naval Base Great Lakes, Illinois

Naval Hospital Great Lakes, Illinois

My experience in Chicago and the surrounding areas was eye-opening for me. Traveling with my four friends was not only safe, but I also learned how to navigate through challenging neighborhoods and bars such as the one we visited in south Chicago. Other options for my off-duty hours included Milwaukee, Wisconsin, located fifty-six miles to the north of the naval base. Travel to this area was easily available via the North Shore line located close to the Naval Base. From our barracks location on base, we could travel to north Chicago, Waukegan Illinois, and other nearby locations for pizza, subs or other fast-food items. On other occasions, we would travel via the North Shore central business area located in downtown Chicago.

Downtown Chicago

The roof dance hall was located at 5th and Wisconsin Ave. Milwaukee Wisconsin. Where a lot of your parents and grandparents went dancing on Friday nights.

One Friday night while returning to the base, an older man in civilian clothes came by the area where we were waiting for a train ride back to the base. He offered a ride directly to the base instead of waiting and then walking from the train station to the main gate. It seemed like a good idea. The three of us, myself, Rick and Don, got into the car. I sat in the back seat with Rick, Don sat up front with the driver.

About fifteen minutes into the drive, Don began to move towards the door and push the driver away from him. Apparently, our driver was making sexual advances that were being denied by Don. This was my first encounter with a homosexual. The remainder of our trip was eventual, and we all learned a life lesson about dealing with strangers.

Throughout my Navy career, I learned much more about homosexuality. Keep in mind that in the 1950's and 1960's, anyone in the military service who was determined to be gay was discharged from the service. This was usually accomplished when naval investigators arrived unannounced at the barracks and escorted the individual from the area never to be seen by his barracks friends again.

A few of my corpsman friends were discharged because of their sexual preference. It was saddening at the time, especially when naval investigators in civilian clothes came into the barracks and escorted my friend away. (*Years later courtroom cases were held to reverse the original findings*). Today we have a blend of homosexuals, bi-sexual, trans-sexual and other classifications including people having surgery to accommodate their sexual preference. Ohio currently has a new law that will require that people must use the restroom based on their birth identity. In other words, men cannot use the girl's restroom, and females cannot use the men's room

Throughout my travels, I have observed gay bars in several countries and the open-mindedness of people around the world. There are also hate groups that people are now aware of, and it is a crime to offend someone who has a different sexual identity than you. When Bev and I were married in 1959, We lived in Philadelphia and attended the Mummers Parade. Which is traditionally held annually in Philadelphia. The parade consists of men dressed up in women's clothes, high-heeled shoes, etc. I was aware of this and informed my 18-year-old wife who was totally in disbelief. This was her first experience in the big city.

In 1959, I had already served four years in the Navy and was now more informed about the ways of life, including sexual variances among the population. Bev was from St Mary's Ohio, and had not been exposed to life's realities. In some instances, newly found ideas became history, such as the Philly cheese steak. It was very popular in the city of Philadelphia, where I had my first Philly cheese steal at the naval hospital in Philly. Philly cheese steaks are now a nationally known food with its roots in Philadelphia.

The ever-popular Philly cheese steak.

My three tours of duty began in 1959 and ended in 1975 when I retired with twenty years of service. Our first house as a married couple was a second-floor apartment located on McKean Street in South Philadelphia, which consisted of a kitchen and living room which doubled as our bedroom.

We purchased a black and white TV for twenty-five dollars. A few months later we moved west to Tasker Housing, nowadays referred to as section 13 housing, or low-income housing.

As a military member with a rank of E-4 (HN), I did not qualify for military housing. Although McKean Street was a friendly Italian American neighborhood, I realized that we needed more space to grow in and Bev was now pregnant with our first child Patty, named after Bev's friend Patricia McArdle. Our move to Tasker Housing provided more living space and was also a friendly neighborhood.

The people living at Tasker housing were low-income individuals with varying ethnicities black, Hispanic, and others. I was attending the Radiology program which at the time was a twelve-month program. Bev used to read my notes and ask me questions about my X-ray topics. After six months of training, I was already taking X-rays at a local hospital.

Before completing the program, I started working part-time at a hospital several blocks east of where we lived. The additional income was helpful in supplementing my pay as an E-4. Our favorite shopping area was the open-air markets on the east side of Philly. Grocery items were always fresh and less expensive than store-bought items.

4th Street Market, Philadelphia

Looking back. I feel that Bev and I have come a long way in terms of maturity and prosperity. For the past five years, I have lived on a six-figure retirement income. We own a beautiful two-story house, with no mortgage and worth over $200,000. We now make donations on a regular basis to help those less fortunate.

On our second tour of duty to the Naval Hospital Philly, I had achieved adequate rank for government (military) housing which was located just down the street from the hospital.

Chapter 2
Hitting the road

There were unusual and sad occurrences on my second tour of duty at the naval hospital. On April 4th, 1968, Martin Luther King was assassinated at the age of 39. He was a Baptist minister and a political activist.

He was known for his contribution to the civil rights movement and gave his most notable speech, "I Have a Dream" at the Lincoln Memorial in Washington, D.C. on August 28th, 1963.

When news of his tragic death reached our neighborhood in Philadelphia, all hell was breaking loose. Unfortunately, one young black man chose to protest by firing a gun into the air. Although unintentional. One of his bullets struck and killed a nearby female civilian. He was tried and found guilty and the last I heard he was serving time in prison. At the Naval Hospital, I had a disagreement with a young black man that escalated, and I was threatened by him. He was court-martialed for threatening someone of a higher rank and was reduced in rank and paid a fine. I felt bad for him and thought the whole thing could have been avoided.

My third and last tour of duty at the U.S. Naval Hospital, Philadelphia was in 1975. We rented a nice home in Marlton, New Jersey, about a 25-30-minute drive. I had to cross the Walt Whitman Bridge on my way home, a very pleasant and scenic drive. We found Marlton to be much more upscale than our previous housing arrangements. I was now a Chief petty officer with a higher income, and we could now visit the more upscale shopping centers. We also had a nice yard to enjoy and a safer place for our kids to play. I bought my first lawn mower here and my next-door neighbor gave me a hand on how to start and use it.

I was also working part-time at the Metropolitan Hospital located near the center of Philly. It paid well and I worked a 7 p.m. to 7 a.m. shift. Eventually, I shared this shift with two other X-ray technicians who were also stationed in Philly. Working a 12-hour shift every third day is much less stressful.

When I worked at the Metropolitan Hospital, I took a different route, crossing the Benjamin Franklin Bridge located farther north than the Walt Whitman Bridge that took me into south Philly, closer to the hospital.

While living in Marlton, New Jersey I was visited by John Stahler. John and I worked together in the Radiology Department at the Naval Hospital. John had a problem with gambling. Unfortunately, his problem had persisted, and he was now without a home. Over dinner, we discussed his predicament, and I agreed to loan him money to help him get back on his feet. He was accompanied by his wife Mary Ann and two young children. During the next week or so, he applied for jobs in Philadelphia and landed a good job in management. He paid me back and found a nice apartment for his family.

I heard From John in a few weeks. Apparently, their pet dog had passed away and John wanted to bury his dog in our backyard. It was a tearful time for John and that was the last time that I saw him. Shortly after this I completed my last tour of duty at the Naval Hospital and moved back to Ohio. I never heard from John again. John was overweight and had some health issues, some I believe he may have passed shortly after our last meeting. Unfortunately, there were no cell phones or FaceBook pages in those days, something I think about on a regular basis.

In retrospect, some of my fondest memories began after leaving the naval base at Great Lakes, Illinois. I was assigned to the Naval Hospital Yokosuka, Japan from 1957 to 1959. I was still a teenager and matured rapidly is this new environment.

The Navy's seventh fleet is headquartered in Yokosuka which in turn impacts the area with thousands of sailors seeking a good time. As a teenager, I experienced several unusual days and nights (working with dead people) as I have outlined in my autobiography "*Looking Back at Me*". I stood guard at the hospital morgue when it was reported that someone was breaking into the morgue and raping female corpses. Also assisted other Navy corpsmen in handling deceased crew members of a helicopter that had crashed. Situations like this help you appreciate the value of life.

I had several sexual encounters with beautiful Japanese women. Although I was paying for sex, as was customary for sailors, the fact that I lived on base instead of a ship classified me as a regular customer. Just having sex costs $1.39 for a "short time". Overnighters cost more, usually around $4.00 to $5.00.

I had stayed overnight with a couple of different ladies and had even attended their place of worship in the morning. They taught me proper etiquette and I was introduced to Shinto and Buddhism, Japan's two major religions. My Japanese neighbors treated me with respect because of the way I was treating my female partners. When I would pass by their residence they would bow and say my name "Buddy San" They knew my name was Buddy since it was tattooed on my arm, plus my girlfriend would introduce me to her friends. San is a polite suffix to a person's name to show respect.

On weekends I would travel with my Corpsman friends John Cambell, Farrel, and a guy named Moose. We attended live stage shows and shopped at Ginza, then known as a very upscale shopping area.

I purchased several souvenirs in this area such as pool sticks. Vases, and carpets, which I placed in a trunk and shipped back to Wapakoneta. Mom and Pete were living in a house trailer near Pete's gas station on Auglaize Street. Pete would eventually move to a better location in downtown Wapakoneta.

Over the years I have remembered my friends and the good times that we shared in Japan. In addition to Tokyo, I spent a few days at a military R and R location located near Mount Fuji. We dressed for the weather and took several photos of our location.

Mount Fuji Japan, era, 1957

From our hotel room, we had a great view of Mount Fuji. This area is now the training grounds for Japan's self-defense force and the U.S. Marine Corps training programs. At the end of my tour of duty in Japan, returned to the United States via a navy ship that was headed for California. The ship's name was the USS *Dixie* (AD-1). Shortly after boarding with three other Hospital corpsmen who were due for discharge from the navy, we were informed that we would all be working in sickbay along with the ship's other corpsmen.

It was an easy transition: working at a brick-and-mortar hospital building with several doctors and nurses to a ship with one doctor and several corpsmen.

Our assignments were easy, assisting the ship's doctor, cleaning, handing out meds, and doing whatever we were asked to do. We crossed the international dateline, which called for a ceremony, with some basic hazing included. It was a very memorable event; however, better memories were yet to come.

The USS *Dixie* pulled into port in Hawaii. The three other corpsmen that I had embarked with quickly made plans to cover the next seven days that we would be in port. We all had similar ideas. Hawaii was well known for its beaches and warm water. Our first move was to share a rental car. From here we found a nearby restaurant and stopped for a nice meal, then onward to our Hawaiian adventure. We drove slowly through the beach area admiring the scenery including the bikini-clad women. We eventually decided to try our hand at surfboarding, observing people who were already participating in this adventure. We each rented a surfboard and casually walked into the water until we were offshore far enough to begin paddling.

Waikiki Beach, Hawaii era, 1959

Waikiki Beach with Mauna Key Mountain

As we sat on the beach area reflecting that we may never pass this way again, at least one guy, possibly two, decided to request permission to be discharged while here in Hawaii. We had heard that the naval station in Hawaii would in fact permit transient sailors to be discharged here in Hawaii since it was now a legal state. When the ship left port, two of our corpsman friends were not onboard. One of the corpsmen who stayed in Hawaii had mentioned that he could use his mustering out pay to buy some surfboards and set up his own business on the beach. I often wonder how he has managed over the years. Since 1959, Hawaii has had tremendous growth and prosperity, especially Waikiki Beach.

The beach area

Chapter 3
Traveling out west

After the USS *Dixie* arrived at the Naval base in San Diego, California, I simply waited in what was called the receiving barracks until my discharge was finalized.

I played pool with other sailors who were waiting for their discharge and had meals provided three times daily in the chow hall. We were informed that there was a bus leaving the base at regularly scheduled intervals throughout the day and returning at scheduled times. Tijuana was only 25 miles south of the naval base and was rumored to be a nice place to visit especially for nightlife and female companionship.

Tijuana, Mexico era, 1959

Sexy Mexican chicks

On the bus ride to Tijuana, a few of the guys mentioned that they had been here before and made a few suggestions. We left the bus in small groups and stayed together just as sailors are taught to do when entering a new or strange port. I still follow this basic rule of safety today. Whenever possible I sit at a table where I can overview the room in terms of who is coming and going through the main entrance.

We did some bar hopping, visited a few shops, and after a few hours headed back to board the bus back to San Diego. After my experience with Japanese and Mexican ladies, it was time to return to Ohio to see if anything had changed and visit with family. I chose to go by rail to look at the country through a train window, instead of flying over it.

My train ride from California went to Chicago, via a train station that I frequented while at the Great Lakes Naval Base. From Chicago, I took a train to Lima, Ohio, only twelve miles from my hometown of Wapakoneta. My sister Aggie and her husband Marion were there to meet me. While at Great Lakes, I also went to Lima by train on weekends and was usually picked up by my older sister Margaret (Aggie). We would routinely stop at our favorite restaurant to get a sandwich. My favorite was the tenderloin sandwich, which appeared to be a local specialty. Tenderloins were found in most bars and restaurants in southwest Ohio.

At this point, I was still single and only owned the property contained in my footlocker (trunk) that had been shipped to Pete's house in Wapakoneta. I had several souvenir items for Mom and Pete. Prior to being away in Japan for the past two years, I had stayed in touch with Angie Nichols, a girlfriend living in Brazil, Indiana. I would date Angie on weekends while I was stationed at Great Lakes, naval hospital. I was alternating my weekends off between taking a train to Lima, Ohio or Terre Haute, Indiana. Angie was a beautiful young lady, and we would spend time at her house watching the Lawrence Welk show on TV.

Lawrence welk show in the 1950's

Shortly after settling in at Pete's house, I decided to drive down to Brazil and visit with Angie. I drove my new 1959 Ford convertible hoping to take Angie out on a long overdue date. I had rented a hotel room in Brazil and shortly after checking in was informed that I had a guest. It was Angie and her sister or lady friend; I do not recall which. Unfortunately, after speaking to Angie, I learned that she was now engaged to someone that she had been working with. I drove back to Wapakoneta, wondering where I had gone wrong and finally settled with the idea that a two-year absence was the problem. I also wondered why she had not informed me of her new boyfriend. Years later I was contacted by her daughter asking me if I was the guy that had visited his dad in Brazil on weekends.

Apparently, Angie's daughter had come upon my Facebook page and sent me a message to see if I was the Bud Hunton they were thinking of. When I confirmed who I was, Angie contacted me and stated that she was very impressed with how my life had turned out. Angie's husband had passed, and I expressed my condolences and sent her a copy of one of my books, and started sending her a card for the Christmas holiday.

Returning to Wapak (short for Wapakoneta), I started seeking employment. I found full-time employment with Omar Baked

Good in Sidney, Ohio, about a twenty-minute drive from Wapak. After much thought, I left Omar within a few weeks and decided to re-enlist in the Navy. Reenlisting for another four years would give me the opportunity to select a service school of my choice, so I chose Radiology. I felt confident that Radiology would provide a more interesting and rewarding career.

I told my girlfriend Beverly of my plans, proposed to her and made plans for our future. We went to Redkey, Indiana and were married on October 24, 1959. Currently celebrating our 65th anniversary.

I had reenlisted through the Navy recruiting office in Lima, Ohio, and was informed that I would be receiving my final orders to the radiology program located at the Naval Hospital in Philadelphia. With my orders in hand, Bev and I headed out In my 1959 Ford with everything we owned in the car. We decided to stop and see my dad and his common-law wife Tina on the way to Philadelphia. Dad was living near Akron, Ohio working as a truck driver. Eventually, he would move to Grove City, Ohio. Dad was well known for his humor among his trucker friends. I would eventually write a book titled "The Life of Harry" one of my best sellers.

On our way to Philadelphia, we stopped to visit with Dad and Tina. They were surprised to see us and were unaware that we had got married. Tina fixed a nice dinner plus a wedding cake in honor of the occasion. In the days to come, we would visit with Dad and Tina when they moved to Grove City, Ohio, less than an hour's drive from our home in Huber Heights, Ohio. The next day we continued our journey to Philadelphia, and at my dad's suggestion, we stopped at his sister Eleanor's house located in North Philadelphia.

Although we were an unexpected company, Eleanor and her husband Freddy were very hospitable. We spent the night before heading to the naval hospital to check in. Uncle Fred was employed as a truck driver, delivering beer throughout the Philadelphia area. He was able to give me detailed instructions to the main gate.

During our future visits, Fred would usually answer the door with a beer in his hand. He was always congenial and friendly. When Dad and Tina came to Philly for a visit, they would invite us to join them at Fred and Eleanors' house where Dad's other sister Mildred and husband George would join us. On various occasions, we would all go to the seashore area. Once I had checked in at the naval base, Bev and found a small apartment on McKean Street in south Philadelphia, and as they say, the rest is history. Twenty years later I retired from the navy and began writing books.

Bev was 18 and I was 21. 1959

My current book count is 10 published, 1 pending.

Once I retired, we moved back to Ohio. I had flown from Philadelphia to Cincinnati for an interview with the administrator of St. Francis Hospital. The interview went well, and they arranged for me to stay overnight and fly back to Philadelphia the next day. My overnight quarters were in an area that used to house nuns from St. Francis.

My employment at St. Francis lasted for less than a year. During my interview, they failed to mention that St. Francis was scheduled to merge with another hospital. I enjoyed my time there with the staff; however, I Interviewed and accepted a job at Grandview Hospital in Dayton, Ohio shortly thereafter, to ensure my future employment.

St. Francis Hospital Cincinnati, Ohio era 1975

Chapter 4
East coast trips

While working at Grandview Hospital, I began writing a monthly column for Advance Magazine out of Valley Forge Pennsylvania. The monthly articles were usually topics I had lectured on at annual meetings and conventions. During my time at Grandview, I also worked part-time as a Radiologic Technologist for Mercy Medical Center in Springfield, Ohio. This was during the time that our region was experiencing a shortage of technologists.

Sinclair College developed a dual track program doubling the number of students in the program. It was at this time that I was recruited by Sinclar. After 21 years at Grandview and 22 years at Sinclair College, I retired for the third consecutive time. Our next adventure was traveling with our daughters and eventually granddaughters to their various games throughout the East Coast.

Great-granddaughters Sophia
and Isabella

Young Sophie

Our two favorite soccer players. Sophie and Bell have been playing soccer ever since they could walk. Coached by their parents who are also soccer coaches, Abby and Andy Mitchell. We have attended their games in several parts of Ohio and were never disappointed at how well they did.

Our grandchildren attended a variety of sports events, soccer, softball baseball, to name a few.

Troy coached various teams of young folks with disabilities, which made us very proud. Here a pictures of Troy pitching for his softball team and a team photo.

Abby Mitchell with her family of soccer players.

Troys manages the team.

Troy pitching softball.

We were now in our retirement years and traveled throughout the country, we attended navy reunions in Branson, Missouri, Charleston, South Carolina, Virginia Beach, Virginia, Jacksonville, Florida, New Orleans, Louisiana, and a few other locations. We traveled to Las Vegas, Nevada twice and also drove west from Vegas to the Grand Canyon Lodge for an overnight stay. The next day we traveled by train up to the Grand Canyon where we viewed nature's most beautiful landscape. I took several photos and included them in my book **"Homeward Bound"** *on the road again.*

Although I have traveled the globe with military friends and family, "there is no place like home" as Dorothy used to say. We have now resided in Huber Heights Ohio for the past fifty years and watched our family grow as we aged gracefully.

A few months ago, we joined the Senior Center in Huber Heights and this will be the final group that I join. Our favorite activity is bingo on Tuesdays, plus group social events provided by the center. In Part 1 of my autobiography, (**"Looking back at Me"**) I did a section with several photos of the senior center.

According to the Harvard Blog, on average, females tend to live five years longer than males. This is visible at the senior center which is attended by more females than males.

Seniors Center, Huber Heights, Ohio

The history of Huber Heights as a community is largely shaped by its history. Huber Heights is located in Wayne Township named in honor of Major General Anthony Wayne. George Washington named him Commander in Chief of the United States Army in April of 1792. The current Seniors Center originated in 1991. Prior to that the previous organization Huber Heights Seniors, Inc. used to meet at the Kitty Hawk school house in Huber Heights from 1984–1990. was the meeting place for seniors. Currently, plans are being made to move the center from its current location to a facility on Shull Road, a building that was previously occupied by Sinclair Community College.

Ironically, I taught at this off-campus location for several years before retiring from Sinclair. Now I am back, sharing my stories with the seniors at the Huber Heights Seniors Center.

Sinclair College Shull Road Huber Heights

The Huber Heights and Englewood branches were both closed after eighteen years of operation. I had taught at the main campus plus off-campus locations.

Navy reunions were held annually. The USS *Robert H. McCard* DD822 was the last ship that served on, 1968–1971. Reunions were held in various states early in the month of October. I have attended several reunions whenever my schedule or health issues permitted. I missed the last one in 2024 due to recovering from Kidney stone issues.

Typical bus tour for reunion attendees.

USS *McCard* returning from Wespac 1968.

The only reunion that I can recall close to Ohio was held at the Cincinnati Hilton Airport, just across the Ohio River in Kentucky. The hotel was about an hour's drive From Dayton, Ohio.

Regardless of location, the selection of hotels was usually very nice, with few exceptions. Rooms were always provided with reasonable prices and very good accommodations. In retrospect, the price paid and the value received was very good.

Cincinnati Hilton Airport

Chapter 5
Traveling on vacation

In addition to traveling to navy regions and with family to various games, Bev and I took vacations to Las Vegas, several locations in Florida, and frequent trips to Pigeon Forge and Gatlinburg, Tennessee. We also spent several weekends in Bown County, Indiana. We could stay at the campgrounds, go horseback riding or stay at a hotel in town and just go shopping. Brown County was an easy three-hour drive from our home in Huber Heights. Vacations in Florida were usually taken during spring break at Sinclair.

One of our favorite locations was a condominium that we rented on Navarre Beach, Florida. We could visit with our cousin Carole and her family in Navarre Beach or drive further south to Lake Placid and visit with sister Jackie and her husband Lee. Each area had good weather compared to what had been experienced in Ohio.

I was able to Vacation while doing distance learning courses from my laptop P. C. While arranging for a week's rental I inquired about the availability of WiFi. I could stay in touch with my students, and grade final exams, all while sitting on our balcony overlooking the ocean.

While staying at the condo, we could also visit with my cousin Carole Cigich who lived ten minutes away. Carole and her husband Ed had both retired and were enjoying their retirement in the area. We would often drive by and take them to dinner. Carole's mother lived with her and Ed. Unfortunately, she passed away a few years after we met her.

Beautiful view of the beach from our condo

While staying at our condo in Navarre Beach, we would usually drive to Pensacola, Florida twenty-five miles west of Navarre. Pensacola was the home of the Navy's Blue Angels and we could see their displays and if the timing was right we could watch them practice. There was also a Navy Exchange where we could do some tax-free shopping.

Carole and Eds house at Navarre Beach Florida
(Bev and Carole on the front porch)

Entrance to Navai Air Station Pensacola, Florida

Home of the Navy Blue Angels

In addition to Pensacola and Navarre Beach, our trips to Florida included Lake Placid to sister Jackie's house or beachfront property owned by one of Jackie's sons. In our years of travel to Florida, I never had to cancel or delay a trip due to weather conditions. In October of 2024, Florida was hit by two major storms, Helene and then Milton. When Hurricane Milton came ashore near Siesta Key Florida, it was said to be the worst storm in that area in the last one hundred years. At least ten people have died and millions are without power. The only explanation I have heard regarding this change is "global warming".

Bev and I have also made trips to other areas in Florida to attend games that our grandkids were participating in. We now tend to stay closer to home for several reasons related to our personal safety. As I have grown older and wiser, I realize my limitations including my medical conditions and needs. I have turned down offers to travel to book signings such as the one in New Jersey, at the McGuire Air Force Base. This offer was a free trip with all expenses paid. I declined due to medical issues including recent issues with a kidney stone and bladder issues.

Closer to home we joined Bevs family at Rustic Haven campgrounds, located south of Grand Lake St. Marys. Our girls were in their pre-teen years and were able to interact with their cousins. Bev's parents and siblings all camped here on weekends. We started by pitching a tent and using sleeping bags. There was a shower house available, as well as outdoor toilets. Eventually, I purchased a house trailer with a few amenities providing a bit more comfort. I also built a small boat dock adjacent to our trailer and eventually added a patio cover so we could sit on our patio deck in the sun. We had a small paddle boat that was enjoyable in the canal area, where the water was safer and more shallow.

Evenings by the lake in a wooded area were very relaxing. We would gather around the fireplace and burn logs, while we roasted marshmallows. During the daylight hours, we could go fishing from the lake bank or boat dock. One of the most favorite fun things to do was go for a pontoon boat ride. My brother-in-law Marion Poppe owned a pontoon boat and accommodated as many people as possible onto the boat. Marion also owned a house trailer located close to ours and owned the fire ring as well. Eventually, my dad Harry Hunton also bought a small house trailer close to ours. Dad's antics and the stories he told were legendary at Rustic Haven. As mentioned previously I would eventually write and publish a book titled "*The Life Of Harry*" which became one of my best sellers.

Family gathering at Rustic Haven Campgrounds.

L-R Pete, Aggie, Bud, Sally, Jackie, Bill and Brenda

It has been fifty years since I retired from the Navy. One of my first accomplishments after retiring was to set up an annual family gathering at the Lake. At first, I just invited family and friends that we spent time with at Rustic Haven. We started with approximately 35-40 people during the first and second years. As word spread, I maintained a list of attendees with names and addresses.

Within a few years, attendance grew rapidly to about one hundred, and I had to rent a shelter house on the east bank of the

Lake. I called the event "Friends and Family Reunion". I would mail invitations out when I had set up the reservation. It was usually at shelter house number one, which provided adequate space for parking, cooking, and playing games. Friends from St. Marys, Wapakoneta, Celina, and several other nearby towns attended. It was a huge success as a carry-in luncheon. People brought their favorite foods and desserts to share or cook.

I decided to buy a door prize to raffle off, such as common household items such as a coffee maker, crock pot, or any other items that were popular at the time. Part of the ticket sales were also used to pay for the shelter house rental.

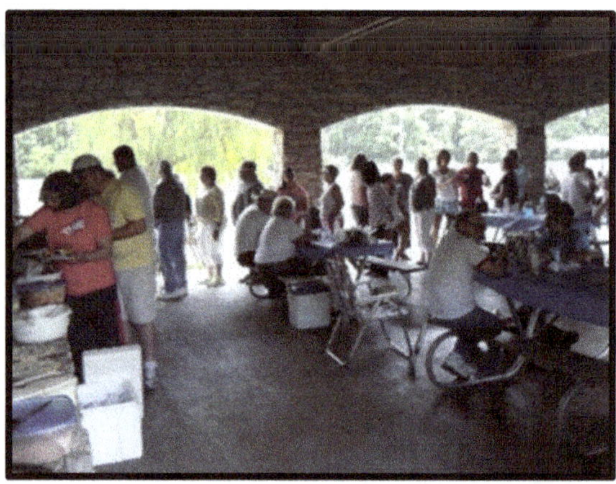

Shelter House No. 1, Family and Friends Reunion.

Sandy and Maggie Goodwin at the reunion

As my workload increased I found it more difficult to manage the task of organizing the event and since there were no volunteers, the event was discontinued. I did assist in setting up other family reunions in the area, on a much smaller scale. The Goodwin family consisted of Frank (doc) Goodwin and his wife Althea, Children: Bruce, Shirley, Sandy, and Margaret (Maggie) Goodwin.

In the year 2024, several of the areas that we used to travel to such as Florida, Virginia, and other states on the East Coast have been affected by extremely bad weather. Hurricane Helene and Milton have devastated multiple states killing several people and leaving many without homes. Hurricane Milton created several tornados wreaking havoc through the middle of Florida.

One of eleven tornadoes caused by Milton

Climate change is the reason for the extreme and violent weather that we are now experiencing across the country. Our out-of-town trips are now determined by the climate changes in various areas of travel. Not only has climate change affected our travel, but increased highway traffic and higher incidents of traffic accidents have occurred. According to a recent news release the local interstate highways in the Dayton, Ohio, Interstate 75 North and South, and Interstate 70 East and West have one of the highest and deadliest accident rates in the country.

In addition to increased traffic, we are also experiencing a repair or replacement of infrastructure throughout the area. These changes have affected our travel via Interstate 75 to Tradersworld, just south of Dayton. Our usual trip time of 35 to 40 minutes has now been increased by 10-20 minutes depending on the time of day.

Traders World flea market located at Monroe Ohio

Traders World is open on weekends from 9 am to 5 pm. Bev and I have traveled to the flea market for several years and have become good friends with some of the vendors. Dick Watson is a well know musician that performs at Traders World on weekends. He usually plays "oldies."

Bev and I with Dick Watson

After our visit to Traders World, we would travel south to the Ikea store located just to the south about a fifteen-minute drive. Ikea was a new store at the time and very popular. I enjoyed their buffet breakfast and lunch. The household items offered were of good quality and value. There were also several outlet malls in the area that we frequented. North from Traders World we could stop by the Dayton Mall, or smaller shopping areas to the east and then go north on Highway 675 towards Route 70 west and on to Huber Heights. At the current time, Bucee's, a nationwide chain of country stores with gas stations Is being constructed in the vicinity of Interstate 70 and Route 235.

As of November 2024, there is currently a dispute regarding whether Huber Heights or Clark County should provide sewer and water services to the future site. Both Bucee and Huber Heights Mayor Jeff Gore reportedly attributed the delay to the Clark County magistrate, who has not made a decision on the services in over 18 months. The company broke ground at the site in August with hopes of being open in late 2025.

Typical Bucees gas stations usually have 120 gas
pumps and a large shopping area.

*Although Huber Heights has grown in size and population over the
last fifty years, the scenery is always beautiful when the seasons change.*

Our home of fifty years.

Route 40 near our home in Huber Heights

As I write my books and think back about past events in my life, I feel blessed to be alive and still have the willpower and energy to continue. In 1976 when we purchased our home in Huber Heights, Ohio there was a small amount of daily traffic that went by our house on Taylorsville Road. So, few cars, that a nearby farm to the west of our house owned horses that they would ride by on a daily basis.

Today. Taylorsville Road is more like an interstate highway with frequent accidents. Route 40 was a primary interstate route before route 70 was created.

Times and places change as we get older. This can be viewed as a negative or positive experience depending on your viewpoint. The old saying. "When life gives you lemons, make lemonade." This saying is attributed to Christian anarchist writer Elbert Hubbard in 1909 in Literary Digest *which reads "A genius is a man who takes the Fate hands him and starts a lemonade stand with them."*

Three of my four daughters (Debbie, Sue and Linda are shown), my oldest daughter Patty resides in Colorado with her husband Ed and two sons Tony and Chris. Pastty's daughter Melissa is on active duty in the Air Force, stationed in New Mexico. We currently have a total of seventeen grand and great-grandchildren.

Photo taken around 2014.

Mother's Day 2023.

On a final note, I proudly present two of my favorite family photos. This photo is several years old and only about half of my family members are present.

I am proud to say that none of our children, or grandchildren have ever been arrested, on drugs or served time in prison. They have all had good jobs and done well with their lives. My wife Bev and I are taking credit for that.

"A hundred years from now it will not matter what my bank account was, the sort of house I lived in, or the kind of car I drove…but the world may be different because I was important in the life of a child."

Forest W. Witcraft teacher, scholar

Changes in our society (from my observations)

- Traffic has increased throughout the United States due to the increase in population and the availability of cars and trucks. Leasing programs now make new cars more accessible and affordable. In 2024 good used cars appear to be less available.
- Auto insurance rates have increased proportionately due to increased accidents.
- The recent law making marijuana legal will also increase accident rates.

Children are now affected by edible cannabis. Recent news reports indicate that hospital Emergency Rooms in Dayton, Ohio are seeing a large uptick in children between the ages of 3-5 years old who have inadvertently eaten candy (chocolate and gummies) that are laced with cannabis. WDTN news reported an increase of 30%. Keep your cannabis products hidden from children and locked in a safe place.

Due to global warming, Hurricanes and tornados have created havoc in several states. A local church collected donations, and I was proud to participate. Unfortunately, the National Weather Service reminds us that these storms will only worsen if do not decrease the amount of carbon dioxide in the atmosphere. Carbon dioxide is a greenhouse gas that traps warm air melts ice caps and creates flooding.

Weather coming from California and the West Coast is known as El Niño, a global coupled ocean-atmospheric phenomenon, the warm phase of the El Nino-southern Oscillation.

Final words

Throughout my three careers since leaving Wapakoneta in 1955, I have not only gained knowledge of the world around me, but, I have also benefitted from the knowledge. Speaking of benefits, although I have been diagnosed with type 2 diabetes, kidney disease, skin cancers, and a few other issues, I have used my medical and dental benefits to pay for most of my medical and dental needs.

Unfortunately, my older brother Harry Hunton Jr. passed away at the age of 59. He had contracted polio in September of 1949 at the age of 14. I was eleven years old at the time and we were living in a rural area just a few miles west of Wapakoneta and healthcare was scarce. Harry (Pete) already had coronary issues before contracting polio which made him a crippled youngster. Today, there are organizations that assist handicapped people. Pete would eventually marry, have a child with his wife Bonnie, and eventually operate a gas station in Wapakoneta.

My older sister Margaret (Aggie) passed away at the age of 88 on September 11, 2024, after a long stay in the area nursing home. She had previously worked at the Good Year plant in St. Mary's, Ohio. Unfortunately, her copays were high so she would often avoid seeing doctors where the copay was more than she could afford. She resided in Florida for a few years after retiring and returned to Wapakoneta to be with her children.

Aggie's three children, Tami, Rick, and Tony still reside in Wapakoneta, Ohio. Tami has been Aggie's caregiver for the past several years as Aggie's health declined.

I've had a great life, and I am no longer a skinny kid with the nickname of "Stump" because of my size. I was 180 pounds at one point in my life, and lost weight due to diabetes injections and went from 38 waist to 34. My first pair of jeans came from my namesake Bud Goodwin. He apparently picked them up while collecting trash in Lima, Ohio.

Overcompensating?

Now that I am in my senior year, I realize that my spending habits regarding men's apparel have been somewhat excessive. We used to have garage sales to eliminate my men's clothing and shoes. People would ask "Who owns all of these clothes?" They may have thought it was a combined garage sale with other neighbors. At the time I could have explained that I had lost a lot of weight and had to purchase new sizes. Regardless, Bev and I eventually turned our spare bedrooms into walk-in closets after our daughters married and left home.

On a positive note, we no longer have garage sales since I started donating excess clothing to organizations such as V.F.W. and other charitable organizations. More recently, we donated clothing and household items to the victims of North Carolina that had been ravaged by Hurricane Helene. At the time of this writing, the death toll from Helene is at 160.

Typical storm damage in western North Carolina created by Hurricane Helene

Donated clothing

Most recent donations. Included upscale clothing
shoes and other items.

Finally, famous quotations to remember when starting out in life:

- "Our prime purpose in this life is to help others. And if you can't help them, at least don't hurt them." —Dalai Lama
- "Life is a series of natural and spontaneous changes. Don't resist them, that only creates sorrow. Let reality be reality. Let things flow naturally forward however they like." —Lao Tzu.
- "Life consists not in holding good cards but in playing those you hold well." —Josh Billings
- "The big secret in life is that there is no big secret. Whatever your goal, you can get there if you're willing to work." —Oprah
- "Never be bullied into silence. Never allow yourself to be made a victim. Accept no one's definition of your life; define yourself." – Harvey Fierstein

Final words and fond memories of:

- My parents: Gertrude Hunton (Childs) and Harry P. Hunton Sr., brother: Harry Hunton Jr. (Pete), sisters: Margaret Ellen Hunton (Poppe), Sally (Sarah) Hunton Jones, Zimmerman, etc., Jackie (Jacqueline Valentine) Hunton, Evans, Rice, Peck.
- Adoptive parents: Bud and Margaret (Mag) Goodwin. Mag was known to the Hunton children as a mum. And Bud was pup.
- Bud Goodwin's brother Frank (Doc) Goodwin and his wife Althea were neighbors with children Bruce, Shirley Sandy, and Margaret (Muggy). Note. My sister Margaret and neighbor Margaret (Goodwin) were both named after Bud's wife Margaret.

Note: During my tenure on earth, I have met several interesting people that I have stayed in touch with such as the Goodwins, and Zimmermans, most recently Bruce Goodwin's daughter Vicky (Goodwin) Jerabek of Carrolton, Virginia.

About the Book

AT THE END OF THE ROAD Part 2 of Bud Hunton's autobiography *is the true story of a young man's experience growing up on a small farm in rural Ohio in the 1940's. Part 2 of Bud's autobiography will focus more on his travels and family values.*

His first home consisted of a log cabin that had been converted into a single-family home without electricity, water or indoor plumbing. His early life was chaotic and unstable with fear of being placed in a foster home. Bud's teen years were worrisome for both him and his parents who would eventually sign the documents to enlist in the navy at 17 years old. This will be Bud's eleventh book that will highlight how to succeed in life when you have an adequate support system.

About the Author

Bud's writing experience began shortly after retiring from the Navy in 1975. During his tenure in the military as a Navy Hospital Corpsman, he traveled the world practicing his medical skills as a Physician's assistant aboard a ship. On shore duty stations (Naval Hospitals), he was a trained Radiographer (X-ray technologist) and had acquired adequate rank and skills to also be a department manager. After retiring from the Navy, he worked at civilian hospitals in Cincinnati and Dayton, serving as department director. While at Grandview Hospital in Dayton, he began writing a monthly column for Advance Magazine out of Valley Forge Pa. His monthly articles were usually topics he had lectured on at annual meetings and conventions.

He was recruited by Sinclair Community College and remained in this position as an instructor for twenty-two years. During this time, he was recruited by McGraw Hill Publishers to assist with editing and writing medical textbooks, including textbooks that were used at Sinclair College such as Basic Medical Terminology. During his time at Sinclair, Bud taught Medical Terminology, Advanced Medical Terminology, and Introduction to Computers. As of October 2024, Bud published ten books, all non-fiction.

AT THE END OF THE ROAD Part 2 of Bud Hunton's autobiography is the true story of a young man's experiences growing up on a small farm in rural Ohio during the 1940s. This second installment will delve deeper into Bud's travels and the importance of family values.

Bud's first home was a converted log cabin, repurposed into a single-family dwelling without electricity, running water, or indoor plumbing. His early life was marked by chaos and instability, coupled with the constant fear of being placed in foster care. Bud's teenage years were equally challenging, causing concern for both him and his parents, who ultimately signed the papers allowing him to enlist in the Navy at 17 years old. This will be Bud's eleventh book, offering insights on how to succeed in life with the support of a strong and adequate foundation.

Bud's writing experience began shortly after retiring from the Navy in 1975. During his tenure in the military as a Navy Hospital Corpsman, he traveled the world practicing his medical skills as a Physician's assistant aboard ship. On shore duty stations (Naval Hospitals), he was a trained Radiographer (X-Ray Technologist) and had acquired adequate rank and skills to also be a department manager. After retiring from the Navy, he worked at civilian hospitals in Cincinnati and Dayton, serving as department director. While at Grandview Hospital in Dayton, he began writing a monthly column for Advance Magazine out of Valley Forge Pa. His monthly articles were usually topics he had lectured on at annual meetings and conventions.

He was recruited by Sinclair Community College and remained in this position as an instructor for twenty-two years. During this time, he was recruited by McGraw Hill Publishers to assist with editing and writing medical textbooks, including textbooks that were used at Sinclair College such as Basic Medical Terminology. During his time at Sinclair, Bud taught Medical Terminology, Advanced Medical Terminology, and Introduction to Computers. As of August 2024, Bud has published nine books, all non-fictions.

ISBN 978-1-966088-58-5